THE MINIATURE BOOK OF

$\mathcal{S}$PICES

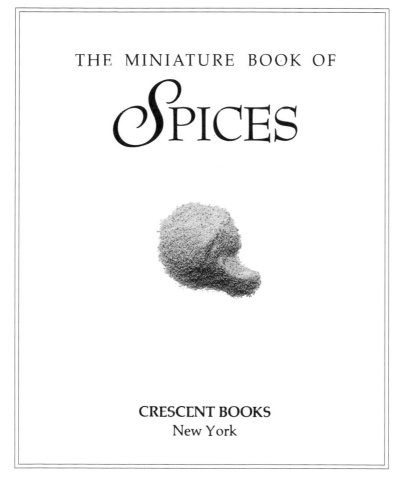

CRESCENT BOOKS
New York

Published by Salamander Books Limited
129-137 York Way, London N7 9LG, United Kingdom

© Salamander Books Ltd., 1991

This 1991 edition published by Crescent Books, distributed by
Outlet Book Company, Inc., a Random House Company,
225 Park Avenue South, New York, New York 10003.

Printed and bound in Belgium

ISBN 0-517-06111-2

87654321

CREDITS

RECIPES BY: *Mary Cadogan, Caroline Cowen, Linda Fraser,
Kerenza Harries, Janice Murfitt, Cecilia Norman, Lorna Rhodes,
Sally Taylor and Mary Trewby*

PHOTOGRAPHY BY: *David Gill, Paul Grater, David Johnson,
Sue Jorgensen, Alan Newnham, Jon Stewart and Alister Thorpe*

DESIGN BY: *Tim Scott*

TYPESET BY: *Old Mill*

COLOUR SEPARATION BY: *P&W Graphics, Pte. Ltd.*

PRINTED IN BELGIUM BY: *Proost International Book Production,
Turnhout, Belgium*

 ONTENTS

$\mathcal{P}$UMPKIN SOUP

1 (3-lb) pumpkin
2 tablespoons butter
1 medium-size onion, chopped
2½ cups chicken stock
1 teaspoon light-brown sugar
⅔ cup half and half
¼ teaspoon paprika
Good pinch grated nutmeg
Salt and pepper to taste
3 slices bread
Oil for frying
Paprika

*D*iscard pumpkin seeds and 'strings'. Cut out pumpkin flesh and dice. Heat butter, add onion and cook until soft. Stir in pumpkin, stock and sugar, bring to a boil then simmer for 30 minutes. Puree vegetables and liquid, return to rinsed pan and stir in half and half, paprika, nutmeg and seasonings. Heat through slowly.

Meanwhile, for the niblets, using 2 cutters, 1 a little smaller than the other, cut out bread rings. Pour a thin layer of oil into a medium-sized skillet, heat. Add bread rings and fry until golden. Drain on paper towels. Sprinkle with paprika. Float on the soup. *Makes 6 servings.*

$\mathcal{M}$ELON &
GINGER SORBET

1 galia melon halved, seeded
²/₃ cup water
¹/₃ cup caster sugar
1 (1-inch) piece fresh ginger root, thinly sliced
¹/₄ cup ginger wine
2 tablespoons orange juice
2 tablespoons lemon juice
Radicchio leaves, to serve
1 oz stem ginger, cut into thin sticks and chervil sprigs
to garnish

*S*coop out melon flesh into a food processor or blender and process to a puree.

In a saucepan, put water, sugar and gingerroot, bring slowly to a boil, stirring. Simmer 3 minutes then cool.

Stir in wine, fruit juices and melon puree. Strain into a freezerproof container, cover and freeze until slushy, about 2 hours. Tip into a food processor or blender and process until soft. Return to container and freeze until firm. To serve, scoop sorbet onto radicchio leaves, garnish with thin sticks of stem ginger and chervil. *Makes 6-8 servings.*

CHILLED FISH SOUP

1 lb unpeeled cooked shrimp
3¾ cups water
2 strips lemon peel
2 bay leaves
2 blades mace
Salt and pepper to taste
4 small prepared squid, cleaned
Green stems 2 green onions, chopped
4 tomatoes, peeled, seeded, chopped
2 tablespoons peeled chopped cucumber

*P*eel shrimp; reserve. Place shrimp shells, heads and tails, water, lemon peel, bay leaves, mace and seasoning in a large saucepan. Bring to a boil, then simmer 3 minutes. Pour through a muslin-lined sieve. Return to rinsed pan. Cut squid into thin rings; chop tentacles. Add squid to pan and simmer 5 minutes. Cool. Add reserved shrimp, green onions, tomatoes and cucumber. Refrigerate at least 1 hour. *Makes 4 servings.*

CLAM SALAD
WITH CHILI DRESSING

1½ lb clams in shells
Salt and pepper, to taste
4 oz small green beans
4 oz button mushrooms, thinly sliced
½ cup pine nuts, thinly sliced
Salad greens
CHILI DRESSING
1 red chili
½ teaspoon fennel seeds, crushed
1 tablespoon lemon juice
¼ cup virgin olive oil
Chervil sprigs to garnish

For the dressing, wearing rubber gloves, remove and discard stem from chili. Halve chili lengthwise, scrape out seeds, finely chop flesh and put in small bowl. Whisk in remaining dressing ingredients, until thickened.

Blanch beans in boiling salted water 2 minutes; drain, refresh under cold running water and drain well. Arrange salad greens on 4 plates. Scatter with beans, mushrooms and clams. Spoon over dressing. Sprinkle with pine nuts and garnish with chervil. *Makes 4 servings.*

SAFFRON CHICKEN

1 packet saffron
1 tablespoon boiling water
2 tablespoon vegetable oil
2 onions, sliced
4 (4-oz) chicken breasts
1 (1-inch) piece gingerroot, finely chopped
4 garlic cloves, crushed
1 dried chili pepper, seeded, finely chopped
1¼ cups plain yogurt
juice ½ lemon
1½ teaspoons sugar
1½ teaspoons salt
1 tablespoon boiling water
Few chives to garnish

*I*n a bowl, put saffron and boiling water; soak 30 minutes. In a large skillet, heat oil. Stir in onions, cook until browned then add chicken breasts. When evenly browned, pour oil from pan; stir in gingerroot, garlic, chili, yogurt and salt. Cover and simmer slowly 20 minutes. Add lemon juice, sugar, salt and saffron with its soaking liquid. Cook, stirring occasionally, over moderate heat to reduce sauce slightly, about 10 minutes. Garnish with chives. *Makes 4 servings.*

CHINESE SPARE RIBS

6 lb lean pork spare ribs, separated
Spring onion tassels to garnish
MARINADE
½ cup hoisin sauce
½ cup miso paste
1¼ cups tomato paste
1½ teaspoons ground ginger
1½ teaspoons Chinese five-spice powder
1 cup muscovado sugar
3 cloves garlic, crushed
1 teaspoon salt
2 tablespoons saki (rice wine) or dry sherry

*T*rim surplus fat from the pork. For the marinade, in a bowl combine marinade ingredients. Place pork spare ribs in a shallow dish and spread marinade over, turning ribs to coat evenly. Cover. Refrigerate at least 4 hours, preferably overnight. Prepare barbecue. Place drip pan over medium hot coals, lay ribs on rack and cook 45-60 minutes until crisp, turning occasionally and brushing with marinade. Garnish with green onion flowers. *Makes 8 servings.*

$\mathcal{D}$UCK &
KUMQUAT SALAD

2 whole duck breasts, skinned, boned, split
About ⅔ cup dry white wine
Pinch of ground ginger
8 coriander seeds, crushed
Salt and black pepper to taste
12 fresh kumquats, sliced
3 tablespoons hazelnut oil
2 teaspoons lemon juice
3 to 4 cups young spinach leaves, washed well, trimmed
½ pomegranate, peel and pith removed, seeds separated

*I*n a large skillet, place duck, wine, ginger, coriander and seasonings. Bring to a boil, then simmer until meat is tender, adding more wine if necessary, about 15 minutes. Add kumquats and simmer 1 minute. Lift meat and kumquats from pan, and keep warm. Reduce cooking liquid by rapid boiling, to ¼ cup. Stir in oil and lemon juice, and heat through. Slice meat, arrange attractively with kumquats and spinach on 4 large plates. Pour warm sauce over, sprinkle with pomegranate seeds, and serve. *Makes 4 servings.*

$\mathcal{M}$USSELS
WITH CUMIN

3 lbs mussels
2 tablespoons vegetable oil
1 large onion, finely chopped
6 garlic cloves, crushed
2 green chilis, seeded, finely chopped
1 (1-inch) piece fresh gingerroot, grated
½ teaspoon ground turmeric
2 teaspoons ground cumin
1 cup water
1¾ cups shredded fresh coconut
2 tablespoons chopped cilantro (fresh coriander)
Cilantro (fresh coriander) leaves, to garnish

*D*iscard any damaged and open mussels. Scrub remaining mussels in several changes of cold water, until clean; pull off 'beards'. In a large saucepan, heat oil in large saucepan, add onion and cook, stirring, until soft, about 5 minutes. Add garlic, chilis, gingerroot, turmeric and cumin. Cook 2 minutes, stirring constantly. Add mussels, coconut and water. Bring to a boil, cover and cook over high heat 5 minutes, shaking pan occasionally, until mussels have opened; discard any that remain closed. Spoon mussels into warmed serving dish, pour liquid over and sprinkle with chopped cilantro. Garnish with cilantro leaves, and serve. *Makes 4 servings.*

$\mathcal{V}$EGETABLE CURRY PARCELS

2 oz puff pastry, thawed
1 egg, beaten
1 teaspoon cumin seeds
Lime twists and herb sprigs to garnish
1 tablespoon butter
1 clove garlic, crushed
1 leek, finely chopped
1 teaspoon garam marsala
1 teaspoon ground cumin
2 teaspoons mango chutney
½ teaspoon finely grated lime peel
2 teaspoons lime juice
½ cup cooked diced potato

For the filling, melt butter in small saucepan, add garlic and leek. Cook over high heat, stirring, 1 minute. Stir in garam masala, cumin, chutney, lime peel and juice. Cook gently 1-2 minutes. Stir in potatoes; cool. Roll out pastry to thin rectangle 12″ x 8″. Cut in 2″ squares and spoon a little filling onto center of each. Brush pastry edges with beaten egg. Draw the corners over filling to meet in center; press joins together. Place on baking sheet. Brush with beaten egg and sprinkle with cumin seeds. Bake in oven preheated to 425F (220C) 5-8 minutes until golden and risen. Garnish. *Makes 24 envelopes.*

$\mathscr{F}$RESH MANGO CHUTNEY

2 mangoes
¼ cup chopped cashew nuts
1 red chili, seeded, finely sliced
¼ cup raisins
2 tablespoons chopped fresh mint
Pinch of asafoetida
½ teaspoon ground cumin
½ teaspoon ground coriander
¼ teaspoon red (cayenne) pepper
Mint sprigs to garnish

*V*ery thinly slice mango flesh. Combine with cashew nuts, chili, raisins and mint. Mix together asafoetida, cumin, coriander and cayenne. Stir gently into mango mixture to coat evenly. Cover and refrigerate 2 hours. Serve cold, garnished with mint sprigs. *Makes about 2 cups.*

$\mathcal{C}$UCUMBER RAITA

½ of large cucumber, sliced into matchsticks
1 cup plain yogurt
1 tablespoon chopped fresh mint
1 green chili, seeded, finely chopped
1 tablespoon chopped cilantro (fresh coriander)
Salt to taste
1 teaspoon cumin seeds
1 teaspoon mustard seeds
Mint leaves or cilantro (fresh coriander) to garnish

*M*ix cucumber with yogurt, mint, chili, cilantro and salt, stirring gently to mix evenly. Cover and refrigerate 30 minutes. Meanwhile, in a heavy skillet, put cumin seeds and mustard seeds. Over medium heat, dry roast until seeds begin to pop, 1-2 minutes. Cool. Sprinkle over cucumber mixture, then refrigerate 30 minutes. Serve cold, garnished with mint leaves or cilantro. *Makes about 1½ cups.*

$\mathcal{A}$SPARAGUS WITH
SESAME & LEMON

1 lb asparagus
4 tablespoons butter
6 green onions, thinly sliced diagonally
Finely grated peel of ½ small lemon
1 tablespoon lemon juice
Salt and pepper to taste
Pinch of red (cayenne) pepper
1 to 2 tablespoons sesame seeds, lightly toasted
1 teaspoon sesame oil
Lemon slices, and sprigs of flat-leaf parsley, to garnish

*T*rim woody, white part of asparagus stems. Cut asparagus spears diagonally in 3 or 4 equal pieces. Cook in a large saucepan of boiling salted water until just tender, 8 to 10 minutes. Drain well. In a large skillet, melt butter. Add green onions and cook over low heat 1 minute. Add lemon peel and juice, then stir in asparagus. Toss lightly until heated through, 2 to 3 minutes. Season with salt, pepper and red pepper. Turn onto a warmed serving platter and sprinkle with toasted sesame seeds and sesame oil. Garnish with lemon slices and parsley. *Makes 4 servings.*

CRAB BURRITOS

1 tablespoon vegetable oil
1 small onion, finely chopped
1 tablespoon tomato paste
1 lb tomatoes, peeled and chopped
1 teaspoon paprika
¼ teaspoon red (cayenne) pepper
2 teaspoons Worcestershire sauce
Salt and pepper, to taste
8 tortillas
2 oz mozzarella cheese, shredded (½ cup)
Shredded lettuce
1 avocado, peeled and sliced
1 tablespoon lemon juice
4 tablespoons dairy sour cream

*I*n a saucepan, heat oil. Add onion and soften. Stir in tomato paste, tomatoes, paprika, cayenne, Worcestershire sauce and seasoning. Boil, then simmer until thick, about 20 minutes. Spread a little sauce over each tortilla, sprinkle crabmeat and mozzarella over, then roll up, tucking in ends. Place in buttered ovenproof dish, and bake in oven preheated to 350F (175C) 20 minutes. Place lettuce on serving plates. Brush avocado with lemon juice then arrange on lettuce. Add burritos topped with tomato sauce and sour cream. *Makes 4 servings.*

SPICED ALMONDS

½ lb shelled almonds
¼ teaspoon ground cumin
¼ teaspoon ground allspice
2 teaspoons salt
3 tablespoons butter

*P*our boiling water over almonds. Leave for 30 seconds, drain. Remove almond skins. In a small bowl, combine cumin, allspice and salt. In a medium-sized skillet, melt butter, add almonds and fry until browned. Drain on paper towels. While hot, toss almonds with spiced salt, to coat evenly. Cool. Place in a sieve and shake off surplus salt. Serve in a small bowl as an unusual accompaniment to cocktails. *Makes 1½ cups.*

COFFEE-CINNAMON CHEESECAKE

 36

CRUST
6 oz chocolate chip cookies, finely crushed
¼ cup unsalted butter, melted
FILLING
2 (8-oz) pkgs. cream cheese, softened
1¼ cups half and half
3 eggs, beaten
¼ cup all-purpose flour, sifted
⅓ cup superfine sugar
3 tablespoons strong coffee
1 teaspoon ground cinnamon
2 (2-oz) squares semi-sweet chocolate, broken in pieces

*F*or the crust, in a bowl, mix cookie crumbs and melted butter. Press into a greased 8-inch springform cake pan. Refrigerate. For the filling, in a bowl, beat together cream cheese, cream and coffee. Beat in eggs, then stir in sugar, flour and cinnamon. Pour onto crust. In a bowl set over a pan of hot water, melt chocolate. Spoon into pastry bag fitted with a fine, plain tip, and pipe over filling. Bake in an oven preheated to 350F (175C) until the filling is set, about 50 to 60 minutes. Cool in oven with door ajar. Remove cheesecake from pan; refrigerate 2 hours. *Makes 8 servings.*

$\mathcal{V}$ANILLA CRÈME BRÛLÉE

4 egg yolks
2½ teaspoons superfine sugar
Pinch of cornstarch
2 vanilla beans
2½ cups whipping cream
Additional superfine sugar
Frosted flowers to serve, if desired

*I*n a large bowl, lightly beat together egg yolks, sugar and cornstarch. With the point of a sharp knife, slit open vanilla beans and scrape seeds into cream. Heat almost to boiling point. Strain onto egg yolk mixture, stirring. Place bowl over a saucepan of simmering water and cook custard, stirring, until thick enough to coat the back of spoon. Pour into individual gratin dishes. Cool, then cover and refrigerate overnight. Two hours before serving, sprinkle a thick, even layer of sugar over top of each pudding. Place under a preheated grill until sugar caramelizes. Refrigerate 1¾ hours. Serve with frosted flowers, if desired. *Makes 4-6 servings.*

39

SPICED APPLE WAFFLES

1 cup self-rising flour
1 tablespoon sugar
¼ teaspoon ground cinnamon
⅔ cup milk
2 tablespoons butter, melted
1 large egg, separated
Grated peel of ½ orange
1 lb cooking apples, peeled and cored
⅓ cup sugar
Pinch ground cinnamon
1 tablespoon butter
Juice of 1 orange
Plain yogurt to serve

*F*or the waffles, in a medium-size bowl, stir together the flour, sugar and cinnamon. Stir in the milk, butter, egg yolk and orange peel to make a smooth batter. Whip egg white to form stiff peaks, then carefully fold into batter.

For the topping, chop apples and place in a large saucepan with sugar, cinnamon, butter and orange juice. Soften over low heat. Brush preheated waffle iron with oil. Fill one side with batter, close lid and cook until no more steam escapes, and waffles are crisp and golden, 2-3 minutes. Remove waffles and keep warm. Serve with topping and yogurt. *Makes 6 servings.*

$\mathcal{L}$EMON &
CARDAMOM CAKE

1 cup ground almonds
⅓ cup superfine sugar
About 3 teaspoons shelled cardamom seeds, ground
½ cup dried bread crumbs
Grated peel and juice of 2 lemons
4 eggs, separated
Pinch salt
Whipping cream and shredded lemon peel to serve, if desired

*S*tir together ground almonds, sugar, cardamom, bread crumbs and lemon peel and juice. Beat egg yolks and add to almond mixture. Whip egg whites until stiff peaks form, then carefully fold into mixture. Pour into buttered 6½-inch springform cake pan and bake in an oven preheated to 375F (190C) until a skewer inserted into center of cake comes out clean, about 40 minutes. Cool in pan, then turn out. Pipe whipped cream on top and sprinkle with shredded lemon peel, if desired. *Makes 6 servings.*

BONOFFEE COFFEE

3 teaspoons instant coffee granules
²⁄₃ cup boiling water
2 cups vanilla ice cream
1 large banana
1¼ cups milk
Few drops vanilla
⅓ cup Tia Maria
2 teaspoons drinking chocolate powder
Chocolate flakes to serve if desired

*I*n a small bowl, stir the water into the coffee. In a food processor or blender, process all ingredients, except the chocolate, until smooth. Pour into cold, tall glasses. Sprinkle tops with drinking chocolate powder, and serve with chocolate flakes, if desired. *Makes 4-6 servings.*